PRESENTED TO

By

Date

Text copyright © 2006 Juliet David
Copyright © 2006 Lion Hudson plc/Tim Dowley
Project Editor: Abby Gough

Published in 2006 by Candle Books (a publishing imprint of Lion Hudson plc).
Reprinted 2006 (twice), 2007 (five times), 2008

Distributed in the UK by Marston Book Services Ltd, PO Box 269, Abingdon, Oxon OX14 4YN
Distributed in the USA by Kregel Publications, PO Box 2607, Grand Rapids, Michigan 49501

Worldwide co-edition produced by Lion Hudson plc,
Wilkinson House, Jordan Hill Road, Oxford OX2 8DR, England
Tel: +44 (0)1865 302750 Fax: +44 (0)1865 302757
email: coed@lionhudson.com www.lionhudson.com

UK ISBN 978 1 85985 602 4

USA ISBN 978 0 8254 7311 1

Printed in Singapore

Candle
BIBLE
for Toddlers

Juliet David
Illustrated by Helen Prole

CANDLE
BOOKS

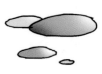

Contents

Old Testament

New Testament

Old Testament

The Beginning

In the beginning there were no people.
No animals. No light. Nothing.

Then God said, "Let there be light."

And there was light. Day and night.
And that was day one.

Next God put water in the sea and clouds in the sky.

And that was day two.

Then God made dry land. And hills.
And rivers. And valleys.

That was day three.

On day four, God put the sun in the sky.

That night the moon and stars came out
for the very first time.

The next day, God filled the sea with fish
and the sky with birds.

That was day five.

On day six God made every sort of animal...

and the first man, Adam.

Everything was just right. Then on day seven God rested!

Adam and Eve

Adam lived in a beautiful garden called Eden.
He named all the animals. What fun!

But Adam was lonely. So God made a woman too, called Eve.

"Enjoy the garden," God said to Adam.
"But never eat fruit from that special tree."

One day a snake slithered up to Eve.
"Why don't you take a bite of *that* fruit?"
"God told us not to," said Eve.

But Eve did bite the fruit.

And then she gave some to Adam, too.

Adam and Eve didn't do as God said, so he sent them out of the beautiful garden.

They were very sorry and very sad.

Noah

Adam and Eve had sons – Cain and Abel.
And then they had children, too.

Soon there were many people on the earth.

But they were unkind and bad.

God was sad. "I shall send a great flood to wash my world clean again," he said.

Then he noticed one good man.
His name was Noah.

God said to Noah, "Build a big boat – bigger than anyone has ever made."

Noah's friends all laughed. "Why are you building a huge boat on dry land?" they asked.

But Noah kept building. When he had finished, God said, "Collect two of every animal."

Then Noah took all the animals and all his family into the ark. And God shut the door.

Then the rain started.

The rain came down and the flood came up!
Soon the ark was afloat on the water.

But everyone was safe inside the ark.

At last the rain stopped and the water started to go down again. Noah sent a dove to find land.

But it came back. It couldn't find any land.

Noah sent out the dove again.

Now it came back with a leaf. Noah knew the dove had found dry land.

The ark came to rest on a mountain. Noah and his family and all the animals came out of the ark.

And God put a rainbow in the sky. He promised never again to flood the earth.

The Great Tower

Men started to build a very high tower.
"Let's try to reach heaven," they said.

God was angry when he heard this. So he made all the people speak different languages.

No one could understand anyone else!

They tried to finish the tower. But because they all spoke in different languages, no one knew what to do next.

So the tower was never finished. And, of course, it never reached heaven!

It was called the Tower of Babel. Or Babble!

Abraham

There was a man called Abraham.

God said to him, "Go on a long journey to a new country." So he set out with his family, his camels, his cattle, and his sheep.

At last he arrived in the land God had promised. There were green valleys and flowing rivers.

Abraham had brought his nephew Lot too. But Lot argued with Abraham. He wanted the best land for his sheep and goats.

"All right, Lot – you take the best land," said Abraham kindly.

God promised Abraham: "One day you will have many children and grandchildren and great-grandchildren in your family."

But Abraham was now very old. And his wife, Sarah, was old. Too old to have children.

One day some strangers visited Abraham. They had a message from God. "You are going to have a son," they promised.

And, sure enough, Sarah had a baby boy.
She named him Isaac.

Isaac grew up to be a fine man.
He helped his father, Abraham.

Abraham sent one of his servants on a journey to find a wife for Isaac.

The servant stopped at a well. God said to him, "The woman who gives water to your camels shall be Isaac's wife."

A young woman came to the well. "Would you like water for your camels?" she asked.

At once the servant knew God wanted her to be Isaac's wife. Her name was Rebekah.

Jacob and Esau

Isaac and Rebekah married and had twin sons.
Esau, the first twin, was very hairy.

Esau liked to go hunting. But Jacob, the second twin, loved to be at home with his mother, Rebekah. He was tricky.

Isaac wanted to give Esau his special blessing.
But Rebekah wanted Jacob to have it instead.

So one day, when Esau was away hunting,
Rebekah put animal skin on Jacob's arms.

By now Isaac was very old and blind. Jacob's arms felt hairy, so Isaac thought he was Esau.

And Isaac gave Jacob his special blessing!

When Esau found out, he was very angry.
"Jacob has stolen my blessing!" he shouted.

So Jacob had to run away to his uncle, who lived in a far country.

One night Jacob lay down to sleep in the desert. He used a stone as a pillow.

He had a wonderful dream. He saw a stairway
to heaven, with angels walking up and down.

When Jacob woke up next morning he said,
"God is in this place!"

At last, Jacob reached his uncle's house. His uncle had two daughters, Leah and Rachel.

Jacob fell in love with Rachel. His uncle told Jacob, "If you work for me seven years, you may marry my daughter."

Seven years later the wedding took place.
The bride wore a veil to hide her face.

But when she took off the veil, Jacob found out he had married Leah – not Rachel.

Jacob still loved Rachel. So he worked seven more years. Then at last he married her.

Many years passed. Jacob decided to go home. He was worried. Was Esau still angry with him?

But when Esau saw Jacob, he gave him a great big hug. The brothers were friends again!

Joseph

Jacob had a big family. He had twelve sons.

Jacob loved Joseph more than his other sons.
He gave Joseph a wonderful coat.

"I dreamt we were in the fields at harvest time," Joseph told his brothers one day. "Your bundles of grain bowed down to mine."

Joseph's brothers were very cross. "So you think
we should bow down to you?" they said.

The brothers plotted against Joseph.
They threw him down a dry well.

Then they sold him to traders. But his brothers told old Jacob, "Joseph has been killed by a wild animal."

The traders took Joseph to the far-off land of Egypt. There they sold him to work for a rich man.

One day, Joseph was suddenly thrown into prison, though he had done nothing wrong!

In prison, Joseph helped people by telling them what their dreams meant.

One night, Pharaoh, king of Egypt, dreamt about seven fat cows. Then seven skinny cows came and swallowed them all up.

Next he dreamt of seven fat ears of grain.
Seven thin ears came and gobbled them all up.

Pharaoh couldn't sleep. He didn't like his dreams.
Whatever did they mean?

Then Pharaoh heard that Joseph was an expert at dreams. He called him to his palace.

"There will be seven years without rain," Joseph explained. "There won't be enough to eat."

Pharaoh was pleased with Joseph. He put him in charge of Egypt. Joseph stored up food so that there was always enough to eat.

And Joseph brought his father and brothers to Egypt so that they had enough to eat too.

Moses

Many years later, after Jacob and Joseph and his brothers had died, a new Pharaoh ruled Egypt.

He was cruel. He made Joseph's family build great temples. Joseph's family were called *Israelites*.

Pharaoh thought there were too many Israelites. So he ordered his soldiers, "Go and kill all their baby boys."

But one woman hid her baby in a basket.

She floated the basket in the river.

Pharaoh's daughter, the princess of Egypt, saw the baby in the basket. She loved him.

So she took the Israelite baby back to her palace. She named him Moses.

When Moses grew up, he ran away from Egypt. He looked after sheep in the desert.

One day he saw a bush on fire. It burned brightly but didn't burn up.

An angel spoke to Moses from the bush. "God says, 'Return to Egypt. Tell Pharaoh to let my people go!'"

So Moses and his brother Aaron went to Egypt.
They told Pharaoh, "God says, let my people go!"

But Pharaoh said, "I don't know your God. And I won't let your people go."

So God made terrible things happen in Egypt.
Frogs hopped everywhere!

Gnats nipped everyone! Flies buzzed everywhere!
Cows got sick and died. The river turned as red
as blood.

People got spots on their skin. Big hailstones fell from the sky. Grasshoppers gobbled the leaves. It was dark everywhere! And the oldest Egyptian children died.

Finally, after all these terrible things,
Pharaoh said, "Go!"

So Moses led the Israelites out of Egypt.
By day, a pillar of cloud went in front.

And at night a pillar made of fire led them.

Then Pharaoh changed his mind! He wanted the Israelites back. So he sent his soldiers to chase them.

The Red Sea was in front. The Egyptians behind.
The Israelites were trapped! They shook with fear!

God told Moses to hold out his stick – and God parted the water.

All the Israelites marched across on dry ground.

But then the waters met again. The Israelites escaped the Egyptian soldiers!

The Israelites spent many years in the desert.
Every morning God sent them special food
called *manna* to collect. It tasted good.

And each night God sent birds called quails to cook and eat.

Moses' Journey to the Promised Land

EDOM

Ezion Geber

MIDIAN

RED SEA

River of Eg...

SINAI
PENINSULA

Wilderness
of Sin

Mount
Sinai

God first
sends manna

Crossing the
Red Sea

River Nile

Memphis

EGYPT

Moses climbed a great mountain called Sinai.
At the top he met with God.

Moses was away so long the Israelites thought he was dead. So they made a calf from gold and bowed down to it.

At last Moses came down the mountain. He carried two stones with God's good rules on them.

When Moses saw the Israelites praying to a golden calf instead of God he was furious.

God told Moses to build a special tent. The Israelites could meet with God there.

Moses was leading the people to the land God had promised. He sent some men to spy it out.

Two men came back with huge bunches of grapes.
"It's a beautiful land!" they said.

But the rest of the spies said, "There are giants in that land. We'll never win it."

Many years passed before the Israelites went to the Promised Land. Moses grew very old and died.

Joshua

God gave the Israelites a new leader.
His name was Joshua.

Joshua led the people across the River Jordan to the Promised Land. They carried the special box from God's tent.

They marched to the great city of Jericho.
How could they ever capture it?

God told Joshua what to do. So the Israelites marched around the city for six days.

But on the seventh day they marched around the city seven times. Then they blew their trumpets and shouted. The walls just tumbled down!

Gideon

Next, God sent a man called Gideon to lead
the Israelites.

God told Gideon, "You need only a tiny army."
Gideon gave his soldiers torches and pots.

At dead of night, Gideon's men smashed the pots and lit the torches.

The enemy soldiers were terrified. They all ran away.
God's people had won!

Samson

God sent a man called Samson to lead the
Israelites. He was very strong.

God helped him kill a lion with his bare hands.

Samson promised God to let his hair grow long. That kept him strong. But then he let a woman cut his hair.

Now Samson was weak. He had disobeyed God.

Ruth

Ruth and her mother-in-law Naomi lived far away. Their husbands had died, so one day Naomi decided to go home to Israel, the Promised Land.

Ruth went too. She wanted to look after Naomi.

One day, Ruth went to the fields to find food for them to eat.

In the fields she met a man called Boaz.
He loved her and they got married.

Samuel

Samuel's mother brought him to the temple.
The young boy was going to help Eli the priest.

One night in bed Samuel heard a voice call, "Samuel, Samuel!"

Samuel ran to Eli. "Why did you call me?" he asked.

"I didn't call," Eli said. "It must have been God."

The boy heard the voice again. "Samuel, Samuel!" This time he listened carefully to what God told him.

When he grew up, Samuel became God's messenger.
The Israelites said, "Give us a king!"

So God sent Samuel to a man called Saul. He poured oil on Saul's head to show that he was king.

At first Saul was a good king. But he began to do things that didn't please God.

So God sent Samuel to find another king.

King David

Samuel visited a man who had eight sons. God chose David, the youngest son, to be king.

One day, David went to fight a giant named Goliath. David had only a sling and five stones.

But David asked God to help him. He swung his sling, a stone hit the giant – and CRASH! Goliath fell down dead.

Sometimes King Saul was grumpy. David played his harp to cheer him up.

David's best friend was Saul's son, Jonathan.

But people said, "David is much braver than Saul."
This made Saul angry. One day he threw a spear
at David.

David ran away. Saul chased him all over Israel.
But God made sure David always escaped.

When Saul died, David became king of Israel.

He and his army beat all Israel's enemies.

David lived in a palace in the beautiful city of Jerusalem.

And he brought the special box
from God's tent to Jerusalem.

David's friend Jonathan had a son called Mephibosheth. He had a bad leg.

David invited Mephibosheth to live in his palace.
He showed him that God loved him.

Wise King Solomon

When David died, his son Solomon became king of Israel.

In a dream God asked him, "What would you like most of all? Money? Health? Food?"

But Solomon said, "Dear God, make me wise."
God was pleased. "You shall be wise," he said.

Solomon the Wise was famous everywhere.
The beautiful Queen of Sheba came from
far away to visit him.

She asked Solomon many questions. Finally she said, "God has made you very wise."

Solomon built a beautiful temple where the people could worship God. Inside, he put the special box from God's tent.

When the temple was finished, people came
from near and far to pray there.

Elijah

Some of Israel's kings were good, like David.
Others were bad, like Saul.

One wicked king, named Ahab, told his people
not to worship God.

God sent Elijah, one of his messengers, to Ahab.
"Tell God you are sorry, or there will be no rain.
No crops will grow. Your people will go hungry."

But Ahab laughed. He did not tell God he was sorry. So it didn't rain.

Ahab was angry with Elijah. He wanted to catch him. So Elijah ran away to the desert. But how would he find food there?

God brought Elijah to a stream where he could drink. And he sent ravens with food to eat.

Later God sent Elijah to a poor woman who lived with her son. "Please give me something to eat," he said.

The woman had only enough flour and oil to make one loaf. But she shared it with Elijah.

"Don't worry," said Elijah. "God will give us food."
After that there was always enough flour and oil.

"God has helped us," said the woman.

King Ahab prayed to an idol called Baal. He asked Baal to send rain. But no rain came.

So Elijah said, "Let's both build an altar from stones."

"Now let's both pray. We'll see if Baal answers."

Ahab and the people prayed to Baal. They danced for him. But still nothing happened.

Then Elijah prayed to God – and fire came from heaven!

And soon rain came too. Now the crops would grow!
The people thanked God.

Elisha

Elijah had a helper called Elisha.

One day, when Elijah was very old, a chariot of fire flew from the sky. It carried him away to heaven.

Elijah threw his coat down to Elisha.

Now *he* was God's special helper.

Naaman

There lived a great army captain called Naaman.
He had a terrible skin disease.

Naaman's servant said, "Go to see Elisha.
He can heal you, with God's help."

So Naaman went to see Elisha. "Dip seven times in the River Jordan," Elisha told him.

Naaman thought this sounded very silly. But his servants said, "Please do as Elisha tells you."

So Naaman dipped himself in the river seven times.

And God healed him.

Jeremiah

God sent more special messengers to the Israelites.
One was called Jeremiah.

"Turn back to God," said Jeremiah. "Or God will send armies from other countries to beat you."

But the people didn't listen. One day, the great king of Babylon came with his army.

He took all the people to his land far away.

Daniel

Daniel was an Israelite. He lived in Babylon, but he still prayed to God.

Daniel was wise. He helped the king of Babylon.

One day the king made a new law.
"Everyone must pray only to me."

But Daniel still prayed to God.
He disobeyed the king.

Then some sneaky men told the king that Daniel was still praying to God.

So the king threw Daniel into a den of lions!

"Dear God, please save me from the lions!" Daniel prayed.

And God shut the lions' mouths. They didn't touch Daniel. He was safe!

Jonah

Jonah was another of God's messengers.

One day, God said to Jonah, "Go to Nineveh. Tell the people to stop doing bad things."

But Jonah was scared. So he took
a boat going the other way.

Suddenly a storm arose. The sailors
threw Jonah into the waves.

God sent an enormous fish to swallow Jonah.
But he wasn't harmed.

After three days, the fish spat him out on the seashore. Jonah learned his lesson!

Now he went to Nineveh as God had told him.

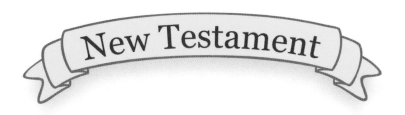

New Testament

Jesus is Born

In a little town called Nazareth lived a young woman called Mary.

One day an angel visited her. "You are going to have a very special baby – God's son," he said. "You must call him Jesus."

Mary was very happy. She sang a song to thank God.

Mary was married to a carpenter called Joseph.
She was expecting her baby soon.

Joseph and Mary had to make a long journey to Bethlehem. Mary was very tired.

There was nowhere to sleep in Bethlehem.
A kind innkeeper said, "Stay in my stable."
So they did.

That night, baby Jesus was born in the stable. Mary made a warm bed for him in a manger.

Shepherds were taking care of their sheep in fields near Bethlehem.

221

Suddenly an angel came to them. "A baby who will save the world has been born in Bethlehem," he told them.

The shepherds were very excited! They rushed off to Bethlehem to find the baby.

They found baby Jesus in the stable. The shepherds told Joseph and Mary what the angel had said.

Far away, some wise men saw a special star.
They followed it to find the newborn baby.

After many days and nights, the star led them
to the little town of Bethlehem.

The wise men gave wonderful presents to baby Jesus: gold, frankincense and myrrh.

Jesus Grows Up

Mary and Joseph took Jesus back to their home in Nazareth.

As Jesus grew up, he helped his parents and played with his friends.

When Jesus was twelve, Mary, Joseph and Jesus went to Jerusalem for a special festival.

Mary and Joseph lost Jesus in the crowds.
They looked for him everywhere.

At last they found him. Jesus was in the temple talking to the priests. They thought he was very wise.

At home in Nazareth, Jesus helped Joseph.
But he knew God had a special job for
him one day.

Jesus is Baptized

A man called John was preaching by the River
Jordan. He told people to stop doing bad
things that made God sad.

Many people said they were sorry. So John dipped them in the river to show they were making a clean start.

Jesus came to the river. He asked John
to baptize him too. And John did.

A dove came from heaven. And God said,
"This is my Son. I am pleased with him."

Jesus is Tested

It was time for Jesus to start his special work
for God. First, he went to the desert to pray.

In the desert Satan came to him. He asked Jesus three trick questions.

But Jesus told him to go away. He said, "The Bible says, 'Don't test the Lord your God.'"

At last Satan gave up trying to trick Jesus.
He left him for a while.

Palestine in the Time of Jesus

River Jabbok

Samaria (Sychar)

Jesus is baptised by John the Baptist

Jericho

Jerusalem

Dead Sea

Bethlehem

Beer-sheba

Jesus Goes to a Wedding

A friend invited Jesus to a wedding. Everyone was enjoying the wine and food.

There's no more wine," said the bridegroom.
"What shall we do?"
"Ask Jesus to help," said Mary.

Jesus said, "Fill the wine-jars with water."
The men did as they were told.

Now the water tasted like wine!
This was Jesus' very first miracle.

Jesus Calls Four Fishermen

One day, Jesus saw four fishermen mending their nets. They were called Peter, Andrew, James and John.

"Follow me," said Jesus. "I will teach you to catch men instead of fish!" And all four went with Jesus.

Jesus Calls a Taxman

People didn't like the taxmen.
They took too much money.

One day, Jesus saw a taxman called Matthew.
"Follow me," he said.

At once Matthew got up, and left his work.
He became one of Jesus' friends.

Then Jesus called some more men to be his special friends.

They were Philip, Bartholomew, Thomas the twin, another James, Simon, Judas and Judas Iscariot.

There were twelve men altogether.
Jesus' special friends, the disciples.

Jesus Makes Sick People Well

Jesus began to travel to many towns
and villages with his friends.

He told people special stories about how God wants the world to be.

One day he climbed a hill. There Jesus taught his friends how to pray.

You should say:
"Our Father in heaven,
Help us to keep your name holy.
Come and be our King
so that everyone here on earth
will do what you want
just as those in heaven obey you.
Give us the food we need today.
Forgive us the bad things we've done
as we forgive those people
who have done bad things to us.
Do not bring us to hard testing
but keep us safe.
Amen

Many sick people came to Jesus. There were people with bad backs and bad legs.

And people who couldn't see or couldn't hear.

Jesus made each one well again.

Jesus Visits a Man at Night

Jesus visited a man called Nicodemus.
He wanted to know more about God.

Jesus said, "You need new life from God!
You must become like a baby all over again."

Nicodemus listened carefully. But he found it difficult to understand.

Jesus Meets a Woman at a Well

One day Jesus sat down beside a well.
He was very tired.

A woman came to fetch water. "Give me some water, please," said Jesus.

Jesus told her lots of wonderful things. She said, "You must be a special messenger from God."

But Jesus said, "I was sent by God to save the world."

The Story of the Good Shepherd

Jesus told many great stories. They all had a special, secret meaning. Here are some of them.

There was once a shepherd who had one hundred sheep. Then one sheep went missing.

At once, the shepherd went to search for the lost sheep. Where could it be?

He searched high and low for his sheep.

At last he found the lost sheep. He put it on his shoulders and carried it safely home.

"Come and have a party with me," he said
to his friends. "I've found my lost sheep!"

Jesus said, "God is happy too when anyone
comes back to God."

The Story of the Two Builders

Jesus told another story, about two men
who decided to build new houses.

The first man built his house on soft sand.

The second man built his house on hard rock.

One day, a storm came, rain fell, and the waters rose.
Soon the house on sand fell down – CRASH!!!

But the house on the hard rock stood firm.

Jesus said, "People who listen to my words, and do as I say, are like the wise man who built his house on rock."

The Story of the Lost Son

Jesus told another story, about a man with two sons.

The younger son decided to leave home.

He went far away. He had lots of parties.
But soon he had no money left.

Now the man had to work. He looked after pigs.
He was so hungry, he ate the pigs' food.

At last, he decided to go home and say sorry to his father.

His father was very happy that his son had come home. He threw a party to celebrate.

Jesus said, "God is happy too when he welcomes home people who were lost."

The Story of the Lost Coin

Jesus told another story, about a
woman who lost a silver coin.

The coin was very special, so she hunted for it high and low.

At last the woman found her lost coin. "Let's celebrate!" she said to her friends. "I've found the coin I lost!"

Jesus said, "The angels are happy like this when a person comes back to God."

Jesus Helps Jairus' Daughter

A man called Jairus had a little girl.
One day she became very ill.

Jairus ran to fetch Jesus.
He wanted Jesus to help.

But when Jesus arrived at the home, Jairus' little girl had died. "Wake up, my dear!" said Jesus.

At once, Jairus' daughter got up and had something to eat. Jesus had done another miracle!

Jesus Calms a Storm

One day Jesus was sailing across the lake with his friends, the disciples. He was tired and went to sleep.

Suddenly a great storm arose. The boat filled with water. The disciples were very frightened.

They woke Jesus. He said "Storm, be still!"
And everything was quiet again.

The disciples were amazed! Even the wind and the waves listened to Jesus.

Jesus Feeds a Great Crowd

Another time Jesus was teaching people all day in the country. They grew very hungry.

Nobody had any food – except one boy. He had five loaves and two fish. He gave them to Jesus, who thanked God.

Then the disciples gave out the food. There were five thousand people – but now there was enough for everyone!

There were even twelve baskets of leftovers.
People were astonished at this miracle of Jesus.

Jesus and the Children

One day some mums wanted to
bring their children to Jesus.

"Go away!" said the disciples.
"Jesus is much too tired."

When Jesus heard this, he said,
"Let the children come to me."

"You will never get into God's kingdom unless you come in like a child," he told his friends.

Jesus and the Tiny Taxman

One day Jesus visited a town where there
lived a tiny tax collector called Zacchaeus.

Nobody liked him because he took more money than he should.

Zacchaeus wanted to see Jesus, but he was just too small. So he climbed a tree.

Jesus saw him and said, "Climb down, Zacchaeus!
I want to come to tea with you."

Zacchaeus changed completely after he met Jesus. He even gave back the money he had stolen.

Ten Sick Men

One day, ten men came to Jesus. They had
a horrible skin disease. "Please help us,"
they asked.

Jesus healed them – all ten.

The men rushed off. They were
so happy to be well again.

Only one man came back. He said, "Thank you, Jesus." But the others completely forgot.

The Blind Beggar

One day the disciples saw a blind beggar.
"Has he done something bad?" they asked.

"No," said Jesus. Then he put
some mud on the man's eyes.

When the man washed his eyes, he could see! Everyone was astonished. Jesus had done another miracle.

Jesus Meets Two Sisters

Jesus met two sisters called Mary and Martha.
They asked him to their home.

Mary sat and listened to Jesus' stories. But Martha was far too busy cooking to listen.

"Come and help me, Mary," said Martha crossly.

"Martha, don't be cross," said Jesus. "Mary has chosen well. She wants to listen to me!"

Down Through the Roof

One day Jesus was teaching in a very crowded house.

Some men wanted to bring their sick friend to Jesus. The house was full. So they climbed onto the roof and made a hole in it.

Then the men let their sick friend down into the room.

The man's friends believed Jesus could heal him.
So Jesus said, "Stand up." And he did!

Jesus Goes to Jerusalem

Jesus decided to travel to Jerusalem again. "Soon I am going to die," he told his disciples. But they didn't understand.

It was festival time in Jerusalem. Jesus borrowed a donkey. He rode it into Jerusalem.

When the people saw him coming, they waved palm leaves. "Jesus is our King!" they shouted.

Jesus Visits the Temple

Jesus went to the temple. Instead of praying, men were buying and selling things there.

Jesus threw them out of the temple. "You are making God's temple into a robbers' den!" he said.

Jesus and the Poor Woman

Jesus watched people put money into
a collecting box in the temple.

Some rich people clanked lots of gold coins in.

A poor woman quietly dropped in two tiny coins. They were all she had.

Jesus said, "She has given more than all the other people." The disciples were surprised.

People Plot against Jesus

Some people in Jerusalem hated Jesus.
They plotted against him.

They gave money to Judas, one of Jesus'
disciples. Then he helped them.

The Last Supper

One night Jesus ate a special supper with his
disciples. He said again, "I'm going to die soon."
But they still didn't understand.

While they were eating, Judas slipped out.
He was going to meet the men plotting
against Jesus.

Jesus took some bread and wine. "Each time you eat bread and drink wine," he said, "remember me."

In the Garden

After supper, Jesus took his disciples to a garden.
"Let's pray here," he said. But they all fell asleep.

Jesus prayed in the garden. It was very dark.

Suddenly, there was a lot of noise!
Judas led Jesus' enemies to him.

Jesus' disciples woke up. They were scared and ran away.

Soldiers arrested Jesus and took him away.

Some people saw Peter watching. "You're one of Jesus' friends," they said.

Peter was very frightened. So he said,
"No – I've never heard of him!"

It wasn't true. Afterwards, Peter was very sorry for what he had said.

A Very Sad Day

Soldiers took Jesus to see the Roman ruler.
He said, "This man has done nothing wrong."

But the people shouted, "Kill him! Kill him!"

So soldiers took Jesus away. They nailed him on a wooden cross and left him to die.

Jesus' family and his friends were very sad.
They had lost a very special person.

Jesus is Alive!

Jesus' friends buried him in a cave. They rolled
a huge stone across the doorway.

But when they came back, the stone had been rolled away. Two angels were inside the cave.

"Don't be afraid," said the angels. "Jesus is alive! He has risen from the dead!"

Two Men Meet Jesus

Two of Jesus' friends were walking home from Jerusalem. They were very sad that he had died.

Another man started to walk with them.
They all talked about Jesus.

When the two men arrived home, they invited the stranger to supper.

As they ate supper, the men suddenly knew
the stranger was Jesus. He really was alive!

The men were so happy! They ran back to Jerusalem to tell their friends.

Breakfast on the Beach

One night, some of the disciples went fishing.

Then they saw Jesus waiting on the beach.
He had lit a fire.

So Jesus had breakfast with his disciples beside the lake. Jesus was alive!

Jesus Goes Back Home

Soon after this, Jesus left his friends.
He returned to his Father in heaven.

But the disciples knew that Jesus was alive forever.

Peter and John Help
a Lame Man

One day, Peter and John went to the temple to pray.

A man sat outside the temple. He couldn't walk. "Please give me some money," he said.

"We have no money," said Peter. "But God will heal you." The man stood up. He could walk!

Peter Escapes from Prison

Peter started to preach to people in Jerusalem. "Jesus is alive!" he said.

But Jesus' enemies didn't like this.
They threw Peter into prison.

That night, an angel came to Peter.
The angel led him out of prison.

Peter knocked on the door of his house.

The girl who answered was so happy to see him that she forgot to open the door!

A Man from Africa Hears about Jesus

A man from Africa was driving his chariot home from Jerusalem. He was reading his Bible. But what did it mean?

Then he met Philip, one of Jesus' disciples. Philip
helped him understand what he was reading.

The man said to Philip, "I would like to be a friend of Jesus too."

Saul Meets Jesus

Saul hated Jesus and his friends.

One day, Saul set out for the city of Damascus to arrest Jesus' friends there.

On the way, a bright light shone. Saul heard a voice from heaven. He fell to the ground.

"I am Jesus!" said the voice. "You're hurting me because you're hurting my friends."

After this, Saul became one of Jesus' friends too. He changed completely. He even changed his name from Saul to Paul!

Paul and Barnabas go on a Journey

Now Paul wanted to tell other people about Jesus.
He made friends with a man called Barnabas.

They walked many miles together. At each place, they told people about Jesus.

Paul Goes to Prison

Later, Paul went to many places with a man called Silas.

In one town, Paul and Silas were thrown into prison. They had done nothing wrong! They had just talked about Jesus.

Even in prison, they sang songs about Jesus all night!

Suddenly, at midnight, the earth shook. The walls cracked. Paul and Silas's chains fell off.

But they didn't run away. The jailer was amazed.
He asked, "How can I follow Jesus too?"

Next day, the jailer set them free. They could go on telling people about Jesus.

Paul Goes to Prison Again

Paul went back to Jerusalem. He was thrown into prison again for being a friend of Jesus.

Paul was taken before the king. "I have done nothing wrong," he said. "I only told people that Jesus is alive."

Paul Sets Sail

Soon after, Paul set sail on a long voyage.

Suddenly a storm arose. The ship was in danger.
But an angel told Paul no one would be hurt.

The winds blew harder. The waves rose higher. Finally, the ship sank.

But Paul and everyone else on board
was safe. They swam to an island.

Later, Paul and Peter and some of Jesus' other friends wrote down everything they knew about Jesus.

Now we can read their stories in our Bible.

The story of Jesus, and how he lived on earth. How he died on the cross and rose again.

And how he lives for ever!